Where Is My Phone?

A 31-DAY DEVOTIONAL TO HELP YOU JUMP
START YOUR DAY WITH JESUS

Write It Out
PUBLISHING, LLC

Norman G. Pierce II and Kizzie Pierce, MDiv

Table of Content

From the Authors

Many Christians often find it difficult to start their mornings with prayer or scripture before rushing off to work, preparing breakfast, or simply beginning the day. Sometimes, it is a matter of not knowing where to start in terms of scripture or what to say in terms of prayer. For many, they pick up their phone and go straight to social media to scroll or see the latest news. For others, it is a matter of hitting the snooze button until the last minute.

The *Where Is My Phone Devotional* is a 31-day guide to remember God at the start of your day. We pray that you will remember this book if you forget your daily morning devotion when you reach for your phone. This book will offer a simple morning devotion that, when read daily, will powerfully jump-start your day. It will only take five to seven minutes out of your morning and ignite a deeper hunger for starting your day with Jesus, even after this 31-day devotional is complete. This book is not published to replace the authentic 66 books of the Bible but as a supplement or a way to jump-start your hunger to read the Word of God. We also give practical stories or words of encouragement with each entry to help you understand each verse given.

May you be encouraged by the simple words of this devotional, and may God strengthen your day with His power as you acknowledge Him first, according to His Word: "In all thy ways acknowledge him, and he shall direct thy paths" (Proverbs 3:6, KJV).

May your heart be strengthened in Christ as you read each day. Remember, though this is a 31-day devotional, you are not in a sprint. If something resonates deeply with a particular season you are in, read it daily and allow the Holy Spirit to minister to you as only He can. We pray that every individual who reads this book will experience the divine power of God daily. Finally, we encourage you to read each entry twice each day. This is a common practice we have learned and taught to others to help them retain what was read. We want you to know that we love you and we are praying for everyone who will read this book.

Sincerely,

Bishop Norman Pierce, II and Lady Kizzie Pierce

About the Authors

Norman G. Pierce II is the founder and pastor of The Real Church in Albany, GA, and serves as a pastor to several senior leaders in the United States and internationally. Born in Savannah, GA, he resides in Albany, GA, or The Good Life City. He holds an associate and bachelor's degree in Business Administration from Grantham University, a bachelor's and master's degree in Theology from North Carolina College of Theology, and a Master of Divinity degree from Beulah Heights University. Additionally, he was awarded an honorary doctorate from St. Thomas University of Jacksonville, Florida, for his philanthropic work in his community and abroad. Bishop Pierce travels extensively, teaching and preaching the Word of God.

Loving, caring, and supportive are three words that describe Kizzie Pierce, affectionately known as Lady P. Born in Alliance, Ohio, Lady Pierce is a nurturing, mighty woman of virtue and integrity. She takes pride in doing ministry alongside her husband, assisting him in his role as founder and lead pastor of The Real Church in Albany, GA, and assisting him as he mentors other leaders. Lady P holds a bachelor's degree in Biblical Studies from North Carolina College of Theology, an associate and bachelor's degree in Religious Studies from Beulah Heights

University, and a Master of Divinity degree from Beulah Heights University. In 2019, Lady P started ShePower Ministries, empowering women to discover the God-given strength within them. She also takes great pride in being a mother, grandmother, and First Lady. She equates much of her spiritual growth to being connected to The Real Church of Albany and her pastor, her husband.

Dedication

This devotional is dedicated to those we affectionately call the Pierce II Clan. This dream has become a reality as Mom and I release our first book. In the early years of our family, we often discussed days like this. Thank you for your unwavering love and support. We have always said, "Through life's challenges, we are in this together." Hands down, we always knew who our first book would be dedicated to. As you read this devotional, may you grow in grace and devotion to God! We love each one of you.

Love,

Mom and Dad

Acknowledgments

We must acknowledge our great church, The Real Church of Albany, GA. We are blessed to be the leaders of such a vibrant church community. Thank you for honoring and loving us as your Senior Pastor and First Lady.

At this juncture, we also want to recognize some amazing inspirations. First, Dr. R. A. Vernon and Dr. Victory Vernon, hands down, our desires for marriage, education, and wholeness are because of your example. Meeting the two of you in 2011 changed our lives tremendously. We are forever grateful for your love and mentorship.

Finally, to the real M.V.Ps, Dr. Julia Berry and Dr. Ruby Grady, your support has been like none other, and blood could not make us any closer. From your love to the moments of stern correction, prayers, and wisdom have always carried us through. You supported us in the worst times of our lives, and even in our lowest places, you always treated us with the utmost respect and honor. In many ways, we stand on your shoulders. This simple acknowledgment is our way of saying thank you. We will always remember who you have been and what you have done in our lives. We pray that before you go to heaven, you see something in us that makes your heart smile, and you know that your labor was not in vain in our lives.

Morning Devotion: Where Is My Phone?

"O God, You are my God; early will I seek You; my soul thirsts for You; my flesh longs for You in a dry and thirsty land where there is no water." –Psalm 63:1 (NASB)

My children spent years trying to get me to move from an Android to an iPhone. My argument was that an Android does the same thing an iPhone does. I know you avid iPhone users will beg to differ, but that was my opinion. Well, finally, I purchased an iPhone as a second phone. I have had it for months. I gave the number to certain people but frequently lost the phone. I received calls from people on my Android, and they'd say, "I called your other phone," to which I'd respond, "I don't even know where that phone is."

We live in a fast-paced world. People are moving quickly to get things done. Some would call it a "microwave society." In our rush, many forget to pray or spend time in the Word. We know we need God, but we have not made Him a part of our day in many ways. The point of this devotional is to encourage you to make an intentional decision to remember God at the start of your day. For many, the first thing we do is grab our phones when we wake up—to check the latest posts on social media, the news, or who liked our previous posts. The list goes on and on. But it is our prayer that you will remember Him every time you pick up your phone. Every time you grab your phone, consider: Have I prayed today? Did I spend time with God or jump out of bed without acknowledging Him?

Many of us have morning routines—some call people first, check emails, or enjoy our coffee. However, none of these things should take the place of God. Nothing can carry you through your day, protect you from harm and danger, or make way for your life. We pray that starting today, as soon as you open your eyes before you do anything, you will grab this book as a supplement only for your Bible and spend time in devotion with the Lord. It is not about how much time you spend with Him, but that you intentionally spend the time. For many, this devotional will be a simple 31-day jump-start. Commit to the 31 days, and watch what God does by the end of it. I pray today marks the first day of a greater hunger for God and that you desire to seek Him early, just as David did in Psalms 63:1, when he said, "Early will I seek You."

Let's Pray:

Heavenly Father, we come before You today, acknowledging that we live in a world that constantly pulls at our attention, but we choose to set our focus on You. Lord, we ask for Your grace to intentionally seek You first every day. Help us to remember that nothing compares to the time we spend in Your presence.

Father, we ask that You would stir within us a hunger for You, a deep desire to start our days with prayer and devotion. Remember that while our phones and routines may be necessary, nothing is more vital than our connection to You. As we pick up our phones each morning, let it be a reminder to pick up Your Word and seek Your face. Guide us through the distractions and busyness of life, and help us to put You first in everything we do.

We thank You for Your constant presence, protection, and provision. Teach us to trust You more, to lean on You for strength, and to walk closely with You throughout our day. We commit these next 31 days to You, Lord, believing that as we seek You early, You will meet us with grace, wisdom, and peace. Transform our hearts and renew our minds as we prioritize time with You. In Jesus's name, we pray, Amen.

Morning Devotion: Commitment To God's Gifts

"From everyone who has been given much, much will be required; and from the one who has been entrusted with much, even more will be expected." –Luke 12:48 (CSB)

God has blessed us with gifts, responsibilities, and opportunities. Because of these blessings, we are required to make an even greater commitment. This commitment isn't a one-time act; it's a daily journey—a daily heart check, a daily spiritual regimen. The key word is "daily."

Our commitment must transcend how we feel in our flesh and even our natural obligations. Too often, we fail in our commitment because we receive the gifts, blessings, and tangible things but don't consider the requirements for maintaining them.

Many know Bishop Pierce loves buying me Brahmin bags. However, even though he purchased them, it's my responsibility to take care of them. Why? Because they're expensive and not your typical purse. The gift was given by Bishop, but it's up to me to honor and appreciate it enough to maintain it. Therefore, I must be committed to caring for them.

In the same way, we must be committed to taking care of God's treasures and the spiritual gifts He has given us. Today, let us be committed to our spiritual walk with God and take care of the things He has entrusted to us. Whether it's your home, vehicle, office, body, or family, today, be intentional about caring for what God has given you, practically and spiritually.

Let's Pray:

Father, in the name of Jesus, we come to You this morning with honor, thanksgiving, and praise. During this time of morning devotion, we approach You with admiration, dedication, and committed hearts. Lord, we thank You for all Your blessings and this new day. We ask You, Lord, to forgive us for all our sins and wash us clean of everything that does not please You.

We come, Lord, thanking You for all the gifts and blessings, both spiritual and natural, that You have given us. We pray that You will help us constantly reflect on these things today and be committed to doing our part to maintain them. Help our children to be committed to learning today. Help all those who will work today to work as unto the Lord. Help us all to be committed to living as Christians today and guide us in doing what is necessary to fulfill these commitments.

Father, we thank You for Your divine commitment to us. Because of this commitment, the devil cannot take us out of Your hands. Today, we commit all of our travel, business, relationships, finances, church family, and leadership into Your hands, according to Your word in John 10:27–30, where You assure us that we cannot be plucked out of Your hand.

We speak blessings and favor over this day for all connected to this time of prayer, and we ask for a special covering over us. We pray for those who have investments in the stock market that their ground will yield fruit. We pray for those who have legal matters to handle this week. We curse worry, anxiety, depression, and oppression, even as a result of poor choices the offender made. We thank You today for good news, blessings, health, and connections. We pray all of this in Jesus's name, Amen.

Day 3

Morning Devotion: Be Still and Trust in God's Timing

"Trust in the Lord with all your heart and lean not on your own understanding; in all your ways submit to Him, and He will make your paths straight." –Proverbs 3:5–6 (NIV)

In our journey of faith, it can be tempting to pursue what we believe is our destiny with all our strength, forgetting that God has a unique plan and timing for each of us. The desire to succeed, to be seen, and to step onto the "stage" we envision for ourselves can sometimes cloud our ability to hear God's voice. But as believers, we must remember that chasing after our plans without consulting God can cause us to miss out on the true inheritance He has prepared for us.

The world may tell us that success is measured in how quickly we achieve our goals, but God's timing is perfect, even when it seems delayed by our standards. When we confuse "not now" with "not ever," we risk taking matters into our own hands, potentially derailing the greater purpose God has set before us. In these moments, we must remember to be steadfast, to trust in God's plan, and to wait on His timing. We are called to be patient, trust, and believe that God works behind the scenes, even when we don't see immediate results.

You don't want to be one of those people who could have gone further if only they had been still. The story of Saul in 1 Samuel 13:8–14 serves as a powerful reminder of this truth. In his impatience, Saul acted against God's instructions, offering a sacrifice that was not his to give, and as a result, he lost the kingdom that could have been his inheritance.

Today, take a moment to pause and reflect. Are you chasing after your own stage? Or are you waiting for the stage that God has prepared for you? Don't miss your inheritance by rushing ahead. Be steadfast, be patient, and trust that God's "not now" is not a "not ever." His plans for you are good and will come to pass in His perfect timing.

Let's Pray:

Heavenly Father, we come before You with a heart that desires to follow Your will above all else. We acknowledge that our understanding is limited, and we often find ourselves eager to pursue our own plans, thinking we know what's best. But today, we will surrender our desires to You, trusting that Your ways are higher and Your timing is perfect. Lord, help us to be steadfast in our faith, even when the path ahead seems uncertain or delayed.

Lord, teach us to be patient and wait for Your perfect timing. When we feel the urge to rush ahead, remind us of Your promise in Proverbs 3:5–6 to trust in You with all our heart and lean not on our own understanding. Help us see what may seem like a delay, but Your loving hand guides us to something far greater than we could imagine. May we be still and know that You are God, resting in the assurance that You are working all things together for our good.

Father, protect us from the temptation to chase after our own stage or seek validation from the world. Instead, may we seek to honor You in all that we do, trusting that the inheritance You have for us is beyond anything we could achieve on our own. Strengthen our resolve to remain faithful, to wait patiently, and to trust in Your divine plan. Let our lives be a testimony of Your faithfulness and grace. In Jesus's name, we pray, Amen.

Morning Devotion: Life Is About Choices

"This is the day which the LORD hath made; we will rejoice and be glad in it." –Psalm 118:24 (KJV)

A choice is selecting or deciding when faced with two or more possibilities. It's a voluntary act that reflects personal preferences, values, and desires. Many people tend to play the blame game instead of owning up to their decisions. It's like the child who, when asked by the teacher why he didn't do his homework, says, "The dog ate it." I even remember when my oldest son, Markel, was in elementary school. He was the child that kept us on our knees in prayer. We would ask him why he misbehaved in school, and he would say, "My friend kept talking to me." Of course, I would ask, "If your friend jumped off a bridge, would you jump too?"

We can even trace this behavior back to biblical times. When Eve ate the forbidden fruit, and God confronted Adam, he blamed Eve. The scripture in Genesis 3:12 says: "And the man said, the woman whom thou gavest to be with me, she gave me of the tree, and I did eat." The core issue is making the right choices and not blaming others. On this day, you must be thankful, praise God, and have a great day, and not allow anything or anyone to hinder you. You are what you choose. The outcome of your situation is what you prefer. Even salvation is a choice.

Today, make a conscious choice to be thankful. Choose not to complain, worry, or fear. Choose to forgive your family, friends, and enemies. Choose to worship instead of throwing in the towel. Tell yourself, "I will rejoice today and be glad," and you can cancel anything and everything that comes to shift that mindset in your day.

Let's Pray:

Father, we praise You for our laying down last night and rising this morning. Lord, we thank You for waking us up with the consciousness of You, Your strength, and the power we need daily.

Your Word says in Psalm 68:19 (KJV): "Blessed be the Lord, who daily loadeth us with benefits, even the God of our salvation." And for this, we say thank You. Father, there is no begging this morning but gratefulness for all that You have done in our lives, for the ways You have moved mountains on our behalf, for the battles You have won that we may never even know about. We also give thanks for the present—what You are doing now, the ways You are shaping us, and the blessings You are pouring into our lives that we may not yet fully see or understand.

We thank You for the power of rejoicing, and today, we choose to rejoice. We cancel anything that could come our way to change that. We thank You for reminding us today of

Your goodness and peace, Your joy and love, and no matter what we face, our hearts will rejoice in You. With the help of the Holy Spirit, we receive an attitude of gratitude, which will be our choice today. In Jesus's name, Amen.

Day 5

Morning Devotion: Every Day Is A New Opportunity

"Because of the Lord's great love, we are not consumed, for his compassions never fail. They are new every morning; great is your faithfulness." –Lamentations 3:22–23 (NIV)

Each day is a gift from God, an opportunity to embrace His new mercies. Yesterday may have been filled with challenges, failures, or even victories, but today is a fresh start. God, in His infinite love, invites us to experience His compassion anew every morning. This means that no matter what we did or did not do yesterday, we have another chance to walk in His grace today.

Lamentations remind us of God's unwavering faithfulness. Life can be unpredictable, but God remains constant. He never gives up on us. His compassions are not tied to our performance but to His steadfast love. It's important to remember that we aren't defined by our past. Every day, Christ presents us with an opportunity to grow, repent, forgive, and trust God more. Think about the beauty of the morning. As the sun rises, it signals the end of night and the beginning of something new. In the same way, God's mercies are like that sunrise— illuminating the path ahead and pushing away the darkness of yesterday's mistakes.

Maybe you feel overwhelmed by yesterday's struggles, but God reminds you that today is another opportunity to rely on Him. You can surrender your fears, burdens, and regrets to God and trust His faithfulness will sustain you throughout the day. As you begin this day, reflect on the opportunities God has placed before you. This is a moment to reset, set new goals, and realign yourself with God's purpose for your life. Let today be a day filled with hope and expectation, whether it's extending grace to someone else, starting a new project, or simply choosing to spend more time in God's presence. God's faithfulness also reminds us to be faithful in return. We can seize the opportunities He provides by stepping out in faith, being diligent in our work, and showing love to others. Let this day be one where you trust God's plan, even if it's unclear. As you move forward, be confident that He will guide you.

Let's Pray:

Lord, we thank You for the new opportunities You provide each day. Help us to walk in Your grace and to trust Your faithfulness, knowing that Your mercies are new every morning. Teach us to embrace the opportunities You set before us with courage and faith. Help us to be a reflection of Your love and compassion for others today.

We surrender our past to You, knowing You are the God who redeems and restores. We release our worries, trusting that You hold our future in Your hands and are bringing everything together for our good. We lay our plans before You, acknowledging that Your plans are higher and better than ours. Guide us in every decision we make, every step we take, and every word we speak. Let Your will be done in our lives, and may we find joy and fulfillment in following the path You have laid out for us.

Thank You, Lord, for Your unfailing love, abundant grace, and constant presence in our lives. We ask all these things in the mighty and matchless name of Jesus, our Savior and King, Amen.

Morning Devotion: The Power Of Self-Denial: Aligning With God's Will

"Then Jesus said to His disciples, 'Whoever wants to be my disciple must deny themselves and take up their cross and follow me."
–Matthew 16:24 (NIV)

In a world that often encourages us to "do you" and prioritize our desires, it's easy to fall into the snare of pride and self-centeredness. Many who embrace this mindset do so out of a place of rejection and a desire to prove their worth. However, as followers of Christ, we are called to a higher standard. Jesus never said, "Do you." Instead, He commanded us to *"deny yourself!"* (Matthew 16:24).

The reality is that much of what we may have attempted in the past may have failed, not because the goals were wrong but because of the heart behind them. When our motivation is rooted in pride, the desire to be seen, or the need to validate ourselves in the eyes of others, any success we achieve will be fleeting. Self-denial, on the other hand, is the key to true greatness. When we deny ourselves and align our hearts with God's will, we don't have to strive to be great—it will happen naturally as God's purpose unfolds in our lives.

Success should not be about fulfilling a twisted desire for importance or creating a narrative we were not called to. Instead, it should operate from a heart that seeks to glorify God in every area—our lives, families, businesses, ministries, and relationships. Remember, self-denial is essential if we genuinely desire to succeed in any area, not for our own glory but for the glory of God.

Let's Pray:

Father, today we come before You in the name of Jesus. We thank You for yet another opportunity to approach Your throne of grace and obtain mercy, for it is Your mercy that we need. We ask for Your forgiveness for the times we have operated out of pride, seeking to elevate ourselves rather than to represent You. Your Word instructs us to deny ourselves, and we acknowledge that we have often failed in this area.

Forgive us, Lord, for what we have done out of our desires to be great, important, seen, and praised by others. While these things in themselves may not be wrong, the motivation of our hearts matters to You. Today, we humbly declare, "No more I, but You be glorified in our lives." May this be true in our families, businesses, finances, ministries, connections, and friendships.

We pray that as we bow our hearts before You, You will bring the necessary changes in our lives. Where pride has birthed things not in alignment with Your will, we ask that You realign those areas according to Your divine purpose. We thank You, Lord, that through the help of the Holy Spirit, we have victory over pride and self-centeredness. May our lives reflect Your glory. In Jesus' name, Amen.

Day 7

Morning Devotion: Waiting On God Is Not A Waste Of Time

*"But they that wait upon the Lord shall renew their strength; they shall mount up with wings as eagles; they shall run, and not be weary; and they shall walk, and not faint." –*Isaiah 40:31 (KJV)

As a child, I often hated asking my parents questions because my mother's response was usually, "Go ask your daddy," and my dad's response was often, "We will see." I was not too fond of both reactions because, in essence, with each one, I had to wait. I would rather hear a "no" than wait. At least with "no," you know where things stand. You can be angry, cry, or vent, but you can move on. With "wait," it's like being left in the balance. This is how life feels at times.

Many of us become frustrated with waiting. Whether it's waiting to get a callback for a job you applied for, perhaps you got the interview and were told you'd hear back, but you haven't heard anything. Maybe you're a single woman waiting for your Boaz to come, but instead, you continue doing life alone. Perhaps you are married and trying for your first child, but despite all your efforts, nothing happens. Whatever the case may be, waiting often does not feel comfortable. But as believers, God always makes the wait worth it.

Don't let the waiting cause you to give up. Just because you are in a season of waiting doesn't mean you should allow it to ruin your day. Get up and seize the day, knowing that God is on your side and He is your guide. Remember His promises: Those who wait on Him will be renewed in strength, and they will mount up like eagles. Waiting is inevitable, but how you wait makes all the difference.

Let's Pray:

Lord, we thank You for this day, for waking us up this morning, and for Your grace. God, we believe in You for so much. There are many things that we are waiting to see become a reality. But Father, we ask You, in Jesus's name, to give us strength as we wait. Sometimes, the answers to our prayers feel so far away, and our faith begins to waver. Our steps grow heavy, and our hearts grow weary. But Lord, we ask You to strengthen us this day as we go throughout our day. Let Your strength be our guide. Please help us to mount up with wings like eagles, soaring above anything that comes to drain our strength. Renew our hope in the waiting, Lord, and let us not grow faint.

Encourage our spirits and remind us that Your timing is perfect. Let our waiting be active and expectant, trusting that You are working, even when we cannot see it. Help us to trust You in the silence, to believe in Your goodness despite delays, and to stand firm in our faith, no matter how long we wait. We know that You are faithful and true, and we place our hope in You, knowing that Your promises will come to pass in due season. In Jesus' name, we pray, Amen.

Morning Devotion: Praise Him

"I will bless the Lord at all times; His praise shall continually be in my mouth." –Psalm 34:1 (KJV)

Good morning, As I prepared today's devotional, my mind returned to a dear woman who meant the world to me, Dr. Idell Cheever. She was the founder and pastor of my childhood church. Dr. Cheever was such a powerful woman of God, and though she has transitioned, she remains an integral part of my life. I would not be who I am today if it had not been for her teachings. She is one of the most vigorous teachers and preachers I have ever known, and I'm blessed to have been pastored by such a great woman and historic figure, being the first woman of many things in my hometown.

Every church has a culture, and in our home church, Pentecostal Miracle Deliverance Center, located in Savannah, GA, we had a culture where, when we greeted someone, instead of saying hello, many would often say, "Praise Him." That was a typical salutation. It wasn't that people were trying to be super deep—they simply had a heart of praise. She taught us that we could praise more out of God than we could beg out of Him. I teach the same principle to The Real Church in Albany, GA, where I am the pastor.

As you wake up this morning, I encourage you to check your heart. Do you carry a heart of praise? Or are you more focused on circumstances that you don't deem favorable? As believers, there should always be praise in your mouth. You may not be able to praise Him for what you are going through, but you can praise Him in what you are going through.

The Bible says in 1 Thessalonians 5:18, "In everything give thanks; for this is the will of God in Christ Jesus for you." Let today be a day of praise for you. As you get up and start your day, let "Praise Him" be your response to adverse circumstances. Let praise be your response to the "no" you wanted to be a "yes." Let praise be your response to the car that cuts you off in traffic. Let praise be your response to the good, the bad, and the ugly. All these things can happen in one day, and if you are not careful, they can make you unbalanced. Therefore, have an attitude of praise all day long, and watch how you end the day in victory.

Let's Pray:

Father, thank You for this day. We come to You praising because You deserve all the praise. We praise You for what You have done and what You will do. We praise You for a successful day. We praise You for giving us the strength to seize the day in victory. We praise You for being our peace in the storm. We praise You for being our shield and our protector. We praise You for every open door and even the doors You have closed for our good. We praise You because Your mercies are new every morning, and Your faithfulness is unending. We praise You for Your unfailing love that sustains us through every trial and tribulation. We praise You for Your grace that empowers us to stand firm in the face of adversity. We praise You for the joy that fills our hearts, even when circumstances are challenging. We praise You for Your wisdom guiding us in all our decisions, for You are our counselor and friend. We praise You for Your provision, meeting every need according to Your riches in glory. We praise You for health in our body, the breath in our lungs, and the ability to move forward in the purpose You have set before us. We praise You for family and friends, for the love and support that You have placed in our lives. We praise You for the gift of salvation, for the blood of Jesus that cleanses and redeems us. Lord, let our lives be a living testimony of praise. Even when we do not understand the "whys," we will still praise You. Even when we cannot see the way forward, we will still praise You because You are the God who makes a way out of no way. We praise You in the valleys and on the mountaintops. We praise You in the quiet moments and in the chaos.

You are worthy of our praise, O Lord, from the rising of the sun to the setting of the same. Your name is great and greatly to be praised. May our hearts overflow with gratitude throughout this day. Teach us to praise You with every word we speak and our actions. Let Your praise rise above every fear, doubt, or worry. Let our praise be a sweet sound in Your ears, O Lord, as we seek to honor and glorify Your name in all we do. In Jesus' mighty name, we pray, Amen.

Morning Devotion: Let It Go

"Forget the former things; do not dwell on the past. See, I am doing a new thing! Now it springs up; do you not perceive it? I am making a way in the wilderness and streams in the wasteland." –Isaiah 43:18–19 (NIV)

In life, we often hold on to things that are harmful to who we are, making it difficult to forget. I strongly dislike the phrase "forgive and forget," as though forgiveness brings amnesia. Forgiveness is not about forgetting but not allowing the same old things to control you anymore. People have deeply hurt me, and my desire was a genuine apology. Well, it never happened. In fact, talking about it seemed to make things worse. Some people will never understand how much they hurt you or how destructive their actions have been to your life. They will never comprehend how you might have been a better version of yourself without the pain they caused you.

Nevertheless, you have a decision to make today—yes, right now. Will you continue to allow the pain of what they did to control you? Or will you decide to let it go? I am not saying it is easy. However, the pain is killing you softly. You are taking your anger out on people who love you and don't deserve to suffer because you suffered in the past. Look at who or what you have become because you won't let it go. Think about this: whatever you decide to hold on to will begin to control you. Subconsciously, we give our enemies power over us when we refuse to let go. Letting go does not mean it never happened. You are not crazy—it did happen. However, it means you will never allow what happened to control your life again.

As you embark upon this day, choose to no longer be plagued by yesterday's trauma. You have talked about it, cried, and received counseling, and the list goes on and on. It's time now to release it and walk into greater.

Let's Pray:

Father God, we come to You today, bringing the weight of past hurts and pains before You. Lord, You know the depths of our hearts and our wounds. We ask for Your strength and grace to release these burdens that have held us captive. We surrender the need for validation and apology from those who have hurt us. Today, we choose to let go of the pain and trust You with the healing of our hearts. Help us, Lord, to walk in freedom. Remind us that we are not defined by the actions of others but by Your love and grace. We release the bitterness, the resentment, and the anger that have taken root in our souls. We forgive, not because it's easy, but because we no longer allow these wounds to control our lives. Father, fill us with Your peace that surpasses all understanding. Strengthen us in our moments of weakness and remind us of the new thing You are doing in our lives. We choose to look ahead and not behind. We trust You, Lord, to make a way where there seems to be no way. As we step into this day, Lord, we ask for Your guidance. Order our steps and lead us along paths of righteousness. Let us approach this day with a heart of joy and expectation, knowing that You are with us in every moment. May Your presence be our peace and wisdom guide our decisions. Help us to respond to others with grace, patience, and love, regardless of what comes our way. Father, protect our minds and hearts as we do our tasks today. Give us the strength to face challenges with courage and the clarity to discern Your will in every situation. Bless this day, Lord, and let Your favor rest upon us. We trust that as we release the past, You are leading us into greater opportunities, new victories, and deeper peace. Thank You for walking with us every step of this day. We trust You with our lives and commit this day to You. In Jesus' name, Amen.

Day 10

Morning Devotion: God Of The Impossible

"Jesus looked at them and said, 'With man this is impossible, but with God all things are possible." –Matthew 19:26 (NIV)

My wife has a saying that I love. She often says, "He is a possible God in impossible situations," I know that to be true. Many people see you where you are but have no idea what you have been through. For example, there was a time in my life when I was homeless. I walked the streets wishing I could find someone to give me $1.05 to get a 99-cent burger from Checkers. I have been through a lot, and most people don't know the half. Some things I caused, while others are a story, which I will share in a book later. A lot of people judged me by my past. It's not that I was so bad; I was growing and learning life from a broken place. Several times, I thought about ending my life, but I knew too much about God to do it. Even when I tried a few times, God didn't let it work. HALLELUJAH! If you knew my life, you would think it was impossible for things to get any better, but God made the impossible possible.

I reflect on the times my family and I struggled to make ends meet. Boy, did we struggle! But we made up our minds that we would not beg or borrow, and we didn't. We fought through with the help of God. At one point, we lived in one of the worst areas of town. We would hit the floor as we heard gunshots. Ramen noodles were a typical meal for my family and me. To this day, I love fried chicken back. We would get a pack of chicken backs for $2.25, and my wife would make a meal out of it. This is not even half of our testimony, but know that God turned things around. He made the impossible possible. I reflect on being very ill—very, very sick. I walk in healing today from what was then because God created the impossible possible.

Here is the point: no matter what you faced yesterday, today is a new day, and no matter how bad it looks, God can turn it around. God can turn it around no matter how many years it has been that way. You may feel like a disappointment. You may not be the who's who of your neighborhood. Maybe the doctor gave you a bad report—all of these things have nothing to do with the power of God. He can change everything in the blink of an eye. You may have been down yesterday and woken up feeling low today... I've been there. But it's in moments like these that you must believe in the power of God. You must know that all you must do is cast your cares on Him and trust Him. All you have to do is be assured that things will get better. Get up today knowing that God will make the impossible possible in your life. The God of the Bible is the God of today.

Let's Pray:

Father God, we come to You in awe of Your power and ability to make the impossible possible. Thank You for the times You have turned our darkest moments into testimonies of Your goodness. We praise You for being the God who sees us, even in our lowest moments, and lifts us up with Your mighty hand.

Today, we cast all our cares, burdens, and impossibilities at Your feet. We trust You to work in the situations that seem too far gone, to restore what has been lost, and to heal what has been broken. Lord, we believe You can turn things around in the blink of an eye. Help us to remain steadfast in faith, trusting that You are working even when we cannot see it. As we go about our day, remind us that nothing is too hard for You. Strengthen our hearts and fill us with hope, even in adversity. May we walk in the assurance that You are the same God who made the impossible possible in the Bible and that You are still doing the same today. We give You all the praise and glory for the victory already ours. In Jesus' name, Amen.

Day 11

Morning Devotion: A Real Friend

"There are 'friends' who destroy each other, but a real friend sticks closer than a brother." –Proverbs 18:24 (NLT)

My first best friend was my older sister, Wanda. It was just the two of us for years, and then our little brother Joshua came along. Wanda was my everything. We laughed, fought, shared secrets, covered for each other, and the list goes on and on. Nevertheless, we had each other's back for real. Even now, we know that if we need each other, we're just one call away.

As I think about my sister, my mind goes to God. How much more is He there when I call? How much more is He, my friend? And why do we subconsciously depend more on natural humans than on the God who made humans? Today, I encourage you—whether you have a great support system or not, whether you are surrounded by people who love you or not, whether you are in a great season or a season that you despise in life or not—Jesus is your friend, and you can always depend on Him to show up.

The old churchy saying goes, "He may not come when you want Him, but He's always on time." Trust Him to move for you. Trust Him to come to your rescue. Trust Him and let Him be your confidant. Let Jesus fight your battles, just like Wanda fought mine. She often told the person I was arguing with, "I know you ain't messing with my little brother." I can imagine Jesus saying the same regarding battles you may face today or tomorrow: "I know you are not messing with My child."

Don't you know Jesus is earnestly your best friend, and He is with you? Perhaps things are rough right now in your marriage or your job; Maybe you are in ministry, and you are experiencing deferred hope. Whatever the case may be, there is a Friend, according to the Bible, who is always by your side. Be conscious about leaning into Him today. Begin your day by telling Him how much you need and want, and trust Him to be your all in all. He loves it when we depend on Him. And as the song says, "He won't let you down, and He won't break your heart."

Let's Pray:

Father, we thank You for being a friend who sticks closer than a brother. You are faithful, dependable, and always there when we call. Today, we choose to lean into You, trusting that You are by our side no matter what we face. Teach us to depend on You more than anyone else and to recognize that You are always on time, even when it seems we're waiting too long. We ask that You help us to be mindful of Your presence today. Let us feel Your closeness and love, especially when we feel alone, discouraged, or overwhelmed. When battles arise, remind us that we don't have to fight them alone—You are our defender, confidant, and ultimate protector.

Thank You for loving us so deeply, never failing us, and being a source of strength and comfort. We invite You to take control of our hearts, our minds, and our situations. Let Your peace surround us, and let Your friendship sustain us. We trust You today, Lord, and we give You all our cares, knowing You care for us. In Jesus' name, Amen.

Morning Devotion: Fulfilling My Desires

"As the deer longs for streams of water, so I long for you, O God. I thirst for God, the living God. When can I go and stand before him?" –Psalm 42:1-2 (NLT)

A few years ago, after some time of pastoring, I remember being at a crossroads. I was tired of how things had been and knew there was more. I remember sitting in the "pulpit," thinking, "There has to be more to ministry than this." I saw people jumping around, shouting, dancing, and singing, but true transformation was often scarce. I couldn't fully explain my feelings then, but I knew it was real. I later realized that I was hungry and thirsty for more. I wanted more of God. I wanted to experience God beyond anything I had before. I was suddenly overwhelmed with the desire for those connected to my ministry to know God beyond religion and tap into an authentic relationship with Him. Soon, that same hunger began to spread to many in our church during that season. Because of that hunger for God, we started seeing real transformations in people's lives.

Here's the point: everything starts with a desire. Do you desire to be better? Do you want more? What do you desire out of your day today? What is the motive behind your desires? Who is at the center of your desires? And what are you willing to do to see those desires come to pass?

Let's Pray:

Father, we come before You today, acknowledging our deep need and desire for more of You. Stir up in us a hunger and thirst for righteousness, Your presence, and a deeper relationship with You. We ask that You align our desires with Your will and purify our hearts so that everything we seek is centered on bringing You glory. Teach us to delight ourselves in You, and as we do, transform our hearts and our lives. Lord, we ask that You remove anything in us that doesn't align with Your purpose. Let our desires not be driven by selfish ambition or worldly gain but by a genuine pursuit of You and Your kingdom.

Father, grant us the strength to push past distractions and focus on what truly matters—Your will being done in our lives. Help us to be patient while waiting and trusting that Your timing is perfect. May we be willing to lay down our plans and expectations, knowing that Your ways are higher than ours. Fill us with Your Spirit, and let that overflow into everything we do.

As we draw closer to You, may we see a transformation not just in our own lives but in the lives of those around us. We ask for Your guidance as we pursue the desires You've placed in our hearts. Help us to trust Your leading and to never grow weary in our pursuit of Your presence. Let our desires bring deeper intimacy with You and empower us to be vessels for Your work. May our lives reflect Your love and grace, and may we always seek to glorify You in all we do. Father, open our eyes to see the opportunities You've placed before us. Give us the courage to step into the unknown with faith, believing that You can do immeasurably more than we can ask or imagine. As we surrender our desires to You, fill us with the joy of knowing that You are at work within us, bringing forth Your good and perfect will. In Jesus' mighty name, Amen.

Day 13

Morning Devotion: I've Got Confidence

"I praise You because I am fearfully and wonderfully made; Your works are wonderful, I know that full well." –Psalm 139:14 (NIV)

There was a time when I avoided interacting with people I perceived as "out of my league." I felt intimidated, insecure, and unworthy of their attention or respect. This self-doubt clouded my perception of who I truly was in Christ. I constantly compared myself to others, believing I could never measure up. But then, one day, God spoke a powerful truth to my heart: *"They are out of your league because you're in your own league."*

This revelation was transformative. It completely shifted how I viewed myself and interacted with others, including my family. God reminded me that I am uniquely made, with a purpose and value that no one else can replicate. I am in his daughter, in a league of my own, not in comparison to others, but as a unique creation of God, fearfully and wonderfully made (Psalm 139:14).

When we understand that we are God's masterpiece, created with intentionality and love, we change the trajectory of our thoughts and actions. No longer do we need to compare ourselves with others or feel inferior in the presence of those we admire. Instead, we can walk in the confidence that comes from knowing who we are in Christ—His beloved children, each with our own calling, gifts, and purpose.

I encourage you to love yourself as God loves you, to embrace who you are in Him, and to grow in confidence, my beautiful people! The world will always try to put us in boxes, to define us by its standards, but God has called us to live according to His truth. He has designed each of us to fulfill a unique role in His kingdom, and no one else can do what you were created to do.

As you walk this journey, remember that confidence is not about pride or arrogance; it's about understanding your worth in God's eyes and living out that identity boldly. Embrace the gifts and talents He has given you, and don't be afraid to step into spaces where you once felt inadequate. God has equipped you with everything you need to succeed in your own lane.

Let's Pray:

Heavenly Father, we thank You for creating us in Your image, fearfully and wonderfully made. Help us to see ourselves through Your eyes, to embrace the person You've called us to be and to walk in the confidence that comes from knowing we are Yours. Lord, guard our hearts against the lies of comparison and insecurity and remind us daily that we are in a league of our own because we are uniquely created by You.

Teach us to love ourselves as You love us, to celebrate the gifts and talents You've placed within us, and to use them for Your glory. When we feel intimidated or out of place, help us to remember that You have called us by name and equipped us with everything we need to fulfill Your purpose for our lives. May we walk boldly, knowing that we are Your masterpiece, created with a purpose that no one else can fulfill.

Father, we ask that You strengthen our hearts and minds, filling us with Your peace and confidence. As we step into new opportunities and face challenges, let us do so with the assurance that we are not alone—You are with us, guiding and empowering us every step of the way. We surrender any fear or doubt to You and choose to trust in Your plan for our lives. In Jesus' name, we pray, Amen.

Day 14

Morning Devotion: Comparison Kills

"For we dare not make ourselves of the number, or compare our-
selves with some that commend themselves: but they measuring
themselves by themselves, and comparing themselves among
themselves, are not wise." –2 Corinthians 10:12 (KJV)

Comparison kills. It slowly drains the joy, peace, and content-
ment from our lives. When we allow our world to be controlled
by comparison, we inadvertently hand over the keys to our
happiness and self-worth to others. We measure our value by
someone else's achievements, appearance, or status, forgetting the unique person God has created us to be.

The reality is that we were never intended to be compared to
others. As I mentioned yesterday, each of us are fearfully and
wonderfully made by God, with our unique gifts, talents, and
purpose (Psalm 139:14). When we compare ourselves to others,
we lose sight of this truth and undermine the beauty of our own
journey.

And listen, not only shouldn't we compare ourselves to others,
but we shouldn't allow those around us to do the same, causing
us to feel like we're less than others. If someone can't appreciate you for who you are, they don't truly understand your worth.

God sees you as His beloved child, and His opinion is the only one that truly matters.

When comparison creeps into your heart, remember this: God has a plan for you that is unlike anyone else's. You don't have to fit into someone else's mold to be valuable or significant. Your life has a unique purpose, and you are equipped with everything you need to fulfill it. It took me a long time to grasp this, but I'm so glad I finally did! I don't have to be like anyone else. What makes me valuable is the fact that I am different.

So, as I have stated before, love yourself! Embrace who you are in Christ and reject the lie that you need to be anything other than what God has called you to be. Surround yourself with people who celebrate you for who you are, encourage you to grow in your own lane, and remind you of your God-given worth.

Let's Pray:

Heavenly Father, thank You for creating us as unique and precious individuals. Help us to resist the temptation to compare ourselves to others, knowing that You have a special plan and purpose for our lives. Remind us, Lord, that our worth is not determined by how we measure up to others but by the fact that we are Your children, loved and valued by You.

Teach us to see ourselves through Your eyes, to love ourselves as You love us, and to walk confidently in the identity You have given us. Protect our hearts from the negative influence of comparison and the opinions of those who do not see our true worth. Surround us with people who uplift and encourage us, celebrate our uniqueness, and spur us on in our walk with You.

Father, we ask for the strength to break free from the chains of comparison and to live in the freedom and joy that comes from embracing who we are in You. May we always remember that we are fearfully and wonderfully made and that You have equipped us with everything we need to fulfill our purpose. Thank You, Lord, for Your unending love and for the confidence we find in You. In Jesus' name, Amen.

Day 15

Morning Devotion: Strength in My Weakness

"But He said to me, 'My grace is sufficient for you, for My power is made perfect in weakness. Therefore, I will boast all the more gladly about my weaknesses, so that Christ's power may rest on me." –2 Corinthians 12:9 (NIV)

As a woman, people often express how they admire my strength to persevere through life's hardships. They usually say things like, "You are so strong" and "I wish I was as strong as you." However, they don't know that I don't rely on my strength to get me through my obstacles, but it is the strength of God. He is the secret ingredient to the recipe for my endurance.

As we begin a new day, it's easy to feel the weight of our limitations. Whether it's physical exhaustion, emotional burdens, or spiritual struggles, we often come face to face with our own weaknesses. Yet, in these moments of vulnerability, God's strength shines the brightest.

The Apostle Paul, a man who accomplished incredible things for the Kingdom of God, openly acknowledged his weaknesses. He understood that admitting his need for God invited God's power to work more fully in his life. Paul's testimony reminds us that our weaknesses are not a hindrance to God's plans; instead, they are an opportunity for His power to be displayed in and through us.

When we come to the end of our own strength, we find that God's grace is more than sufficient. His power is not just available but perfected in our weakness. This signifies that when we feel inadequate, overwhelmed, or insufficient, God steps in and provides exactly what we need. He gives us the strength to face challenges, the wisdom to make decisions, and the peace to remain steady in the midst of turmoil.

As you go about your day today, don't be discouraged by your limitations. Instead, bring them before God and allow Him to work through them. Let His strength become your strength. Trust that He will carry you through whatever you face and that His grace is more than enough for every situation. Remember, we accomplish great things not by our might or power but by the Spirit of the Lord working in us.

Let's Pray:

Heavenly Father, as we start this day, we come before You, acknowledging our weaknesses and limitations. There are moments when we feel inadequate, overwhelmed, or unsure of the path ahead. But we take comfort in knowing that Your grace is sufficient for us and that Your power is made perfect in our weakness.

Lord, we ask that You fill us with Your strength today. When we feel weak, remind us that we can lean on You, for You are our ever-present help in times of need. Help us see our weaknesses not as obstacles but as opportunities for Your power to be displayed in our lives. Teach us to rely entirely on You, trusting that You will provide everything we need to face the challenges of this day.

Father, let Your strength carry us through every difficulty and let Your peace guard our hearts and minds in Christ Jesus. May our lives be a testimony of Your power working through our weakness, and may others see Your grace and love reflected in all we do. We surrender this day to You, trusting in Your unfailing love and perfect plan for our life. In Jesus' name, we pray, Amen.

Morning Devotion: Breaking Free From Negative Expectations

"For as he thinks in his heart, so is he." –Proverbs 23:7a (NKJV)

Sometimes, the way we are wired can be our biggest obstacle. We may find ourselves in a pattern of expecting negativity, especially when things are going well. It's as if we've been conditioned to believe that something terrible must follow every season of joy or success. Listen, I've been there! This mindset is not just unhealthy; it's a trick of the enemy to keep us from fully embracing the blessings and peace that God wants us to experience.

Warfare is real, and life certainly brings challenges, but many of the difficulties we face can be traced back to our own "stinking thinking." If we continually expect negativity, we set ourselves up to attract it. Our thoughts are powerful, and they shape our reality. Proverbs 23:7 says, *"For as he thinks in his heart, so is he."* This implies that our mindset and expectations play a significant role in what manifests in our lives.

It's time to break free from the cycle of expecting defeat and start embracing the victory that is ours in Christ Jesus. You can live a happy, fulfilled life. Something wrong does not have to happen just because you're experiencing a great season. Instead of waiting for the other shoe to drop, declare that you are victorious, blessed, and protected by the power of Jesus Christ.

Remember, defeat is not an option when you are in Christ. The enemy may try to sow seeds of doubt and fear, but you can stand firm in the knowledge that God has already secured your victory. Declare over your life that you are blessed, and expect good things to happen. Release your mind from negative thinking and embrace the abundant life that Jesus has promised you.

Let's Pray:

Father, today we come before You with a heart full of gratitude. We thank You for bringing us to the realization that we are victorious in You. Lord, we ask for Your forgiveness for allowing "stinking thinking" to dominate our minds. Help us fully comprehend that we have victory in every area of our lives in You. Defeat is not our portion.

Today, we decree and declare that we walk in the blessings of God. Our families are blessed, our lives are blessed, and our finances are blessed. We reject the lie that we are under attack because we are covered by the blood of Jesus. Father, we thank You for the open doors that bring greater opportunities into our lives and household. We praise You because we cannot be stopped, sidetracked, trampled over, or discouraged by the enemy, for our lives are committed and hidden in You.

Lord, we declare that we are free from sickness, disease, viruses, and any other physical ailments. We are free from generational curses, for they are not our portion. By faith, we proclaim that we are free from any and all curses because of the sacrifice made at Calvary. Lord, we praise You that our minds are alert and our hearts are fixed on You. Nothing can pull us away from Your purpose.

When the enemy comes to bring us down, we trust that You will fight for us. You will stand up for us, and the Spirit of the Lord will rise like a flood, preventing any negative force from reaching us. Father, we release our minds from "stinking think-ing" and any thoughts that paralyze our lives. We release from our mind thoughts of failure, struggle, lack, evil overtaking us, regression, being hurt, betrayal, loneliness, poverty, sickness, divorce, and premature death. All these things are far from us, in Jesus' name, Amen.

Day 17

Morning Devotion: The Importance Of Discernment: Guarding Your Heart

"Above all else, guard your heart, for everything you do flows from it." –Proverbs 4:23 (NIV)

Sometimes, to avoid being judgmental, we open our hearts or circles to people who may ultimately cause harm. Despite the warning signs, our desire to give others a chance can lead us to make decisions that bring pain and regret. In 2023, I experienced something deeply hurtful. Despite knowing what I sensed in my spirit and being aware of this person's past, I chose to dismiss my discernment and take a chance on them. I thought to myself, "Well, someone took a gamble on me."

Here's the lesson I learned: Never turn off your discernment or ignore wisdom in the name of being non-judgmental or giving someone a chance. Someone may have given you a chance, but it's important to remember that you didn't have the same heart or destiny as the person in question. There is a difference between being open-hearted and being unwise. Having healthy boundaries or a wall up is not always negative, especially when it stems from a pure heart and a desire to protect what God has entrusted you.

As believers, we are called to be as wise as serpents but as harmless as doves (Matthew 10:16). This implies using God's discernment to navigate relationships and situations. Wisdom and discernment are gifts from God that help us protect our hearts, our peace, and our purpose. Ignoring these gifts can open us to unnecessary warfare, pain, and disappointment.

Trust your discernment and, at the very least, listen to wisdom. Remember that a leopard doesn't change its spots unless God intervenes. Discernment is not about being judgmental; it's about being cautious and wise, recognizing that not everyone has the same intentions or calling in life. Be vigilant and protect the purity of your heart, but do so without becoming paranoid or closing yourself off from the possibility of genuine, healthy relationships.

Let's Pray:

Heavenly Father, as we begin this day, we come before You with a heart that seeks Your wisdom and guidance. We thank You for the gift of discernment that You have placed within us and ask that You sharpen it even more today. Help us to walk in Your wisdom and guard our hearts with diligence, knowing that everything we do flows from it.

Lord, we pray that You protect us from any influences or connections not aligned with Your will for our lives. Give us the strength to listen to Your voice, even when it's difficult, and to trust the promptings of the Holy Spirit. Forgive us for the times we have ignored Your guidance or allowed ourselves to be led by emotions rather than by Your truth.

Today, we release any hurt, bitterness, or resentment from past experiences. We choose to walk in forgiveness and love, knowing that You are our shield and our defender. Teach us to be wise as a serpent yet harmless as a dove, as Your Word instructs. May we approach every relationship and situation with a heart full of Your love and the wisdom to know when to step back and protect our peace.

Father, we ask that You surround us with people who will uplift and encourage us and help us to be a blessing to others. Let our discernment be a tool for building up, not tearing down. Keep us humble, Lord, and remind us that true wisdom comes from You alone.

Thank You for the new mercies of this day and for the assurance that You are with us in every decision we make. We trust that You will guide our steps, protect our hearts, and lead us in the way everlasting. In Jesus' name, we pray. Amen.

Morning Devotion: Walking In Love: Reflecting God's Compassion

"And above all these put on love, which binds everything together in perfect harmony." –Colossians 3:14 (ESV)

Love is the cornerstone of our faith and the essence of Christ's teachings. In Colossians 3:14, we are called to *"put on love,"* which binds all virtues together in perfect harmony. This love is not merely an emotion but a deliberate choice to act in kindness, compassion, and grace toward others. Walking in love means allowing our actions to reflect the heart of God and embracing every opportunity to extend His love to those around us.

Every day brings new opportunities to walk in love, but it also presents challenges that test our ability to embody this love genuinely. Whether it's in our interactions with family, friends, colleagues, or even strangers, our response should be grounded in the love Christ demonstrated. By choosing to act with love, we align ourselves with God's will and become a living testament to His goodness and mercy.

Walking in love requires intentionality and surrender. It means letting go of personal grievances and choosing to forgive as Christ forgave us. It involves serving others selflessly and showing compassion even when it's challenging. Love is a powerful force that can break down barriers, heal wounds, and bring hope to a hurting world. Will you walk in love today?

Let's Pray:

Lord, we come before You with a heart full of gratitude, thanking You for the new opportunities You graciously provide each day. Your love and faithfulness are unending, and we are humbled by how You continually guide and sustain us. Help us, Lord, to walk in Your grace and to fully trust in Your faithfulness, especially when we face challenges or uncertainties. Your Word reminds us that Your mercies are new every morning, and we stand on this promise, knowing that each day is a fresh start, filled with possibilities that You have ordained.

Teach us, Father, to embrace the opportunities You set before us with courage and faith. When we are tempted to shrink back in fear or doubt, remind us that You are with us and that all things are possible with You. Strengthen our resolve to step out in faith, even when the path ahead is unclear. Help us to trust in Your wisdom and to lean not on our own understanding but to acknowledge You in all our ways, confident that You will make our paths straight.

Lord, we ask that You help us to be a true reflection of Your love and compassion to those we encounter today. May our words, actions, and thoughts be aligned with Your heart, bringing encouragement, hope, and kindness to others. Let us be a vessel of Your peace in a world that so desperately needs it.

When others look at us, may they see You, and may our lives be a testament to Your goodness and grace.

We surrender our past to You, knowing You are the God who redeems and restores. We release our worries, trusting that You hold our future in Your hands and are working all things together for our good. We lay down our plans before You, acknowledging that Your plans are higher and better than ours could ever be. Guide us in every decision we make, every step we take, and every word we speak. Let Your will be done in our lives, and may we find joy and fulfillment in following the path You have laid out for us.

Thank You, Lord, for Your unfailing love, abundant grace, and constant presence in our lives. We ask all these things in the mighty and matchless name of Jesus, our Savior and King, Amen.

Morning Devotion: The Joy of Serving Others

"For even the Son of Man came not to be served but to serve, and to give his life as a ransom for many." –Mark 10:45 (ESV)

Service is at the heart of the Christian life, modeled perfectly by Jesus Christ. In Mark 10:45, Jesus reveals the essence of His mission on earth: He came not to be served but to serve. This selfless act of service was not just about meeting physical needs but was a profound expression of love and sacrifice. By giving His life as a ransom for many, Jesus demonstrated the ultimate act of service and set a powerful example for us to follow.

Serving others brings a unique and profound joy beyond worldly pleasure. When we serve, we align ourselves with Christ's purpose and experience a deeper sense of fulfillment. This joy arises from knowing that our actions reflect God's heart and contribute to His kingdom work. Service allows us to step outside of ourselves and focus on the needs of others, fostering a spirit of humility and love.

In a world that often values self-promotion and personal gain, embracing a life of service can be countercultural. Yet, it is in serving others that we find our true calling and purpose. No matter how small, acts of service create ripples of kindness and compassion that can profoundly impact others and draw them closer to God. Each time we extend a helping hand, lend a listening ear, or offer a word of encouragement, we embody Christ's love and reflect His character.

Growing up in church, I often found myself serving in different areas of ministry, from transportation to ushering to assisting with cleaning the church, etc. I served in whatever capacity was needed. I never considered until recently the magnitude of my servanthood and the impact it has had in my community and my local church. I truly believe it has made me the woman I am today.

As we serve, it's important to remember that our motivation should not be for recognition or reward but for genuine love and a desire to honor God. In Philippians 2:3-4, we are instructed to *"do nothing from selfish ambition or conceit, but in humility count others more significant than yourselves. Let each of you look not only to his own interests but also to the interests of others."* This perspective transforms our approach to service, turning it into a joyful act of worship and gratitude.

Let's Pray:

Heavenly Father, we thank You for the incredible example of service Jesus set for us. His willingness to give His life as a ransom for many inspires us to live a life of service and humility. Help us to reflect His love and compassion in our interactions with others.

Lord, we pray that You would open our eyes to the needs around us and give us a heart eager to serve. Teach us to find joy and fulfillment in putting others before ourselves and to embrace opportunities to serve with a willing and cheerful spirit. May our actions be driven by genuine love and a desire to honor You, not for our recognition but to glorify Your name.

We ask for Your guidance in every act of service we undertake so that we might be a true reflection of Your grace and kindness. Let our lives be a testimony to the joy that comes from serving others, and may we experience the deep satisfaction that comes from aligning our hearts with Your will.

Thank You, Lord, for the privilege of serving and the joy it brings. May we continue to follow in Jesus' footsteps, serving others with humility and grace. In Jesus' name, Amen.

Morning Devotion: Complete In Him: God's Plan

"Being confident of this very thing, that He who has begun a good work in you will complete it until the day of Jesus." –Philippians 1:6 (NKJV)

The journey of faith is marked by continual growth, transformation, and trust in God's promises. Philippians 1:6 provides a profound assurance that the work God begins in us is significant and steadfast. Paul's confidence is rooted in the belief that God, who initiates the good work in our lives, will faithfully complete it. This assurance is crucial as we navigate the ups and downs of our spiritual journey.

When Paul speaks of the "good work," he refers to the transformative process of salvation and sanctification. From the moment we accept Christ, God begins a work of renewal, healing, and purpose in our lives. This work is not about immediate changes but involves a lifelong process of becoming more like Christ. It includes spiritual growth, character development, and fulfilling God's purposes in us.

One of the most comforting aspects of this verse is the promise that God will complete His work. It's easy to feel discouraged when we don't see immediate results or continuously struggle with ongoing issues. However, Philippians 1:6 reassures us that God's work is not contingent on our efforts or perfection. He is committed to bringing about His plans and purposes in our lives. The process may be long and challenging, but we can be confident that God is at work, shaping and preparing us for His plan.

I often reflect on my past experiences, from childhood to adolescence. Although it didn't feel good at the time, I can now see how God was working in every area, whether good or bad. My experiences have made me a better wife, mother, first lady, daughter, and, above all, a better human being. I know that there is still more that God is working in me. After all, he must finish what he started. Know that He is doing the same for you.

Let's Pray:

Heavenly Father, we thank You for the promise in Philippians 1:6 that You who have begun a good work in us will complete it. We are grateful for Your faithfulness and the assurance that You are at work in our lives, even when we cannot see the progress.

Lord, help us to remain confident in Your plan and purpose, even during times of struggle and uncertainty. Teach us to trust You fully and to embrace the process of change with patience and faith. When doubts arise, and we feel discouraged, remind us of Your promise and the truth that You are committed to completing the work You have started in us.

As we navigate through unanswered questions and challenging situations, grant us the wisdom to testify of Your past faithfulness or prophesy with hope about what You will do. Strengthen our resolve to remain steadfast and trust in Your timing and plan.

Thank You, Lord, for Your unwavering commitment to us and the confidence we can have in Your promises. We place our trust in You, knowing that You are always at work and that Your plans for us are good. In Jesus' name, Amen.

Day 21

Morning Devotion: Faith Over Fear: Embracing God's Peace

"For God has not given us a spirit of fear, but of power and of love and of a sound mind." –2 Timothy 1:7 (NKJV)

Life often brings situations that can make us feel afraid or uncertain. These feelings can sometimes overwhelm us, whether it's fear of the future, worries about our circumstances, or anxieties about things we can't control. But the Bible reminds us in 2 Timothy 1:7 that fear does not come from God. Instead, He gives us power, love, and a sound mind.

Fear is a normal reaction to the unknown; we all experience it at different times in our lives. However, God calls us to respond to fear with faith. He wants us to trust Him, even when things are unclear or challenging.

"Faith over Fear" became a famous phrase for many believers during the COVID-19 pandemic. As the world faced unprecedented uncertainty, anxiety, and fear, this phrase served as a reminder to trust in God's sovereignty and goodness, even in the midst of a global crisis.

Choosing faith over fear means trusting that God is in control, no matter what. It's about believing He has a good plan for our lives, even when we can't see it. When we feel afraid, we can remember that God is with us and has given us the strength to overcome any fear.

Living with faith over fear doesn't mean we'll never be afraid; however, it does mean that we can face our fears with confidence, knowing that God's power is greater than anything we might face. We can pray and ask God for His peace and guidance, trusting He will lead us through whatever challenges come our way.

Let's Pray:

Heavenly Father, we come before You with grateful hearts, thanking You for the precious promise that You have not given us a spirit of fear but of power, love, and a sound mind. We are so thankful for Your unwavering presence in our lives, especially during times of uncertainty and anxiety.

Lord, when we are faced with fear, whether from the challenges of our circumstances or the unknowns of the future, help us to remember that You are always in control. Remind us that nothing happens outside of Your knowledge and care, and You are our refuge and strength, an ever-present help in times of trouble.

We ask for Your divine strength to rise above the fears that try to take hold of our hearts and minds. Empower us with Your Spirit to choose faith over fear daily, trusting in Your perfect plan and timing. Help us cast our anxieties on You, knowing You care deeply for us.

Thank You, Lord, for Your constant faithfulness. We surrender our fears, doubts, and worries to You and ask that You replace them with Your peace, strength, and love. We are confident that with You by our side, we can face anything that comes our way. In Jesus' name, Amen.

Day 22

Morning Devotion: His Love Never Fails

"For I am convinced that neither death nor life, neither angels nor demons, neither the present nor the future, nor any powers, neither height nor depth nor anything else in all creation, will be able to separate us from the love of God that is in Christ Jesus our Lord."
–Romans 8:38–39 (NIV)

One of the most reassuring truths in scripture is that nothing can separate us from the love of God. In Romans 8:38-39, Paul emphatically declares that no matter what we encounter—whether life's greatest trials or the unknowns of the future—God's love remains steadfast and unbreakable.

Rosa, our youngest child, is a teenager. If you've ever raised a teenager, you know that they often think they know more than you about life and this world we live in. There have been times while communicating with her over the phone, I've had to correct her, and even though she is aggravated, she will always make sure she says, "Bye, love you." Honestly, there were moments when she was more adamant about saying it than I was.

Although she is human, she is an example of how God regards us. This passage serves as a powerful reminder that God's love is not dependent on our circumstances, our feelings, or even our actions. His love for us is rooted in His very nature, and it is demonstrated most clearly through Jesus Christ. Because of what Jesus accomplished on the cross, we have been brought into a secure, eternal, and unchanging relationship with God.

When life throws its hardest challenges at us—whether sickness, loss, fear, or doubt—we can stand firm in the knowledge that God's love surrounds us. It's easy to feel isolated or abandoned when things aren't going well, but this scripture reassures us that nothing, absolutely nothing, can tear us away from His love.

God's love is stronger than any force we might encounter. It is more powerful than the most daunting circumstances and more enduring than the deepest trials. No matter where we find ourselves—on the mountaintop of joy or in the valley of despair—His love is always present, holding us close and guiding us through.

In those moments when we feel unloved or unworthy, let us remember that God's love is not something we have to earn or deserve. It is freely given and ours forever because of Christ Jesus, so let this truth sink deep into your heart: His love never fails.

Let's Pray:

We come before You with hearts full of gratitude for Your unshakable love. Thank You for the truth that nothing can separate us from Your love, no matter what we face in life. Your love is our foundation, our refuge, and our strength.

Lord, we ask for Your help remembering this truth when facing life's challenges. When we feel overwhelmed, remind us that Your love is constant and unbreakable. Help us to trust in Your love, even when circumstances make it hard to see.

Forgive us for the times we've doubted Your love or felt unworthy of it. Remind us that Your love is a gift, given freely through Jesus Christ and that we are secure in this love forever. Fill our hearts with peace and joy, knowing nothing can tear us away from You. We pray that we will live out this love in our daily lives. Teach us to love others as You have loved us and to be a reflection of Your grace and kindness in the world. May our lives be a testimony to the power of Your love, drawing others closer to You.

Thank You, Lord, for loving us with a love that never fails. We surrender our fears, doubts, and worries to You and rest in the promise of Your unending love. In Jesus' name, Amen

Day 23

Morning Devotion: Praise Is What I Do

"I will bless the Lord at all times; His praise shall continually be in my mouth." –Psalm 34:1 (NKJV)

Praise is more than just a physical act of worship; it is a life-style, a constant expression of gratitude and reverence toward God. In Psalm 34:1, the psalmist declares a commitment to bless the Lord at all times, meaning that praise is not reserved for moments of joy and victory alone but also for times of struggle and difficulty.

During our worship experiences at church, my husband often says, "We can praise more out of God than we can beg out of Him." When we choose to praise God in every situation, we shift our focus from our circumstances to His greatness. Praise is a powerful act of faith, a declaration that we trust God even when things don't make sense. In these moments of praise, we align our hearts with God's truth, reminding ourselves of His faithful-ness, goodness, and sovereignty.

As long as we praise God, we have no room for complaining. Whether on the mountaintop of success or walking through the valley of challenges, praise keeps our hearts connected to God. It keeps us grounded in the truth that God is in control and wor-thy of our worship regardless of our circumstances.

Praise is what we do, not because everything is perfect, but because God is perfect. It is an act of obedience, a response to who God is and what He has done in our lives. Even in times of pain, confusion, or loss, we can still lift our voices in praise because we know that God is with us, He is for us, and He is working all things together for our good.

When we praise, we invite God's presence into our situation. We make room for His power to move in our lives. As we lift our praise, God lifts our spirits, giving us the strength to keep going, the peace to rest in Him, and the joy that comes from knowing we are His.

Let us make praise a daily practice, not just in the good times but in all times. From this day forward, allow praise to be the first thing on your lips in the morning and the last thing in your hearts at night. Let it be your response to every blessing, every trial, every moment of our lives. After all, praise is what we do because that's what we were created for.

Let's Pray:

Heavenly Father, we come before You with hearts full of praise. You are worthy of all our worship, adoration, and love. Thank You for being a constant presence in our lives, for being our refuge, strength, and comfort in every situation.

Lord, we declare today that praise is what we do. We choose to bless Your name at all times, not just in moments of joy but also in times of struggle. Help us to keep our focus on You, even when life is challenging. May our praise rise to You like incense, a pleasing aroma that brings honor to Your name.

We ask for Your help in cultivating a heart of praise. When we feel overwhelmed by our circumstances, remind us to lift our eyes to You. Fill our mouths with songs of thanksgiving and our hearts with a deep sense of gratitude for who You are and all that You have done.

Lord, we pray that our praise will be a testimony to those around us. Let it be a light in the darkness, a source of hope and encouragement to others. May our lives be a reflection of Your goodness and love, drawing others closer to You through our witness.

Thank You for the privilege of praising You, the joy it brings, and the way it draws us nearer to Your heart. We love You, Lord, and we praise You today and always. In Jesus' name, Amen.

Day 24

Morning Devotion: Believing God's Truth Beyond Life's Facts

"And you shall know the truth, and the truth shall make you free."
–John 8:32 (NKJV)

As believers, we are called to live by faith, not sight. This means that our faith is not anchored in life's shifting circumstances but in the unchanging truth of God's Word. Life may present certain facts that can be daunting, discouraging, or even devastating. However, God's truth always stands above these facts, offering us hope, strength, and freedom.

Consider the facts that life may present to you: a diagnosis from the doctor, financial struggles, or a sense of failure in your endeavors. These facts are real, and they may weigh heavily on your heart. But as children of God, we are not bound by the facts of this world; we are liberated by the truth of God's Word.

The fact may say you are sick, but God's truth declares that by His stripes, you are healed (Isaiah 53:5). The fact may say you are broke, but God's truth assures you that He will supply all your needs according to His riches in glory by Christ Jesus (Philippians 4:19). The fact may say you are defeated, but God's truth proclaims that you are more than a conqueror through Him who loves you (Romans 8:37).

In John 8:32, Jesus tells us that knowing the truth will set us free. This freedom comes from aligning our thoughts, words, and actions with God's truth rather than the temporary facts of our situation. When we know the truth—genuinely realize it in our hearts—we are no longer bound by fear, doubt, or despair. Instead, we can freely live in the victory Jesus has already won for us.

This doesn't mean we ignore the facts of life or pretend they don't exist. Instead, it means confronting these facts with the higher truth of God's promises. We acknowledge what is happening in the natural, but we stand firm in the supernatural truth that God is greater than any challenge we face.

Believing God's truth over life's facts requires faith—faith that God is who He says He is and that He will do what He has promised. It's about trusting in His character, His power, and His love, even when the facts seem to tell a different story. When we choose to believe God's truth, we experience the freedom that comes from knowing that He is in control and that His plans for us are good.

So today, whatever facts you are facing, remember that they do not have the final say. God's truth does. Stand on His promises, declare His truth over your life, and walk in the freedom that comes from knowing His truth will always prevail.

Let's Pray:

Heavenly Father, we thank You for the truth of Your Word that stands above every fact we may face in life. Thank You for the promise that Your truth sets us free. Today, we choose to believe Your truth over the facts that life presents to us.

Lord, help us to walk by faith and not by sight. When we are confronted with difficult circumstances, remind us of Your promises. Give us the strength to declare Your truth over our lives, even when the facts seem overwhelming.

We ask for Your wisdom to discern between the facts of our situation and the truth of Your Word. Teach us to trust in Your character and love, knowing that You always work for our good.

Father, we surrender our fears, doubts, and anxieties to You. Fill us with Your peace and the confidence that comes from knowing that Your truth never changes. We stand on Your Word today and proclaim that we are healed, provided for, and victorious in Christ.

Thank You, Lord, for the freedom we have in Your truth. May we walk in that freedom each day, living in the fullness of Your love and grace. In Jesus' name, Amen.

Day 25

Morning Devotion: We Die Daily

"I affirm, by the boasting in you which I have in Christ Jesus our Lord, I die daily." –1 Corinthians 15:31 (NKJV)

1 Corinthians 15:31, Paul profoundly states: "I die daily." This phrase summarizes the daily surrender required of every believer—a willingness to lay down our desires, our will, and fleshly impulses to follow Christ more closely.

What does it mean to die daily? It means choosing to crucify our flesh with its passions and desires (Galatians 5:24). It's an intentional act of setting aside our own ways of thinking, our ambitions, and our comfort to pursue God's will. This daily dying is not just a one-time event but a continual process that refines us, shapes us, and molds us into the image of Christ.

Dying daily is not easy. It means letting go of our need to control, our fear of the unknown, and our attachment to the things of this world. It means saying "no" to the temporary pleasures that our flesh craves and "yes" to the eternal joy that comes from walking in obedience to God. It's a daily decision to live for Christ rather than for ourselves.

I often quote those three words as a reminder that flesh is a mess. It's just like taking a shower/bath. Though you may take one in the morning, by the evening time, whether you see it or not, you have become dirty again. Just like we must continue to shower/bath to stay clean, this is the same as our spiritual walk with God. Each day brings on new challenges, but in order to overcome them, we must be willing to die to our ways.

Dying daily also means embracing humility. It's recognizing that we are not the center of the universe but that Christ is. It's about placing God's desires above our own and seeking His glory in all we do. This daily death allows us to grow in grace, be more patient and loving, and be like Jesus in our interactions with others.

As we die daily, we find that we are being renewed inwardly day by day (2 Corinthians 4:16). The old is passing away, and the new is coming to life. This process of dying and rising is the essence of the Christian walk—a journey that leads us closer to God and deeper into the life He has called us to live.

So today, let us embrace the call to die daily. Let us surrender our will to God's, knowing that in doing so, we are stepping into the fullness of life that He has for us.

Let's Pray:

Heavenly Father, we come before You today with hearts willing to surrender. We acknowledge that we are called to die daily, to lay down our own desires, and to follow You with our whole hearts. Help us, Lord, to embrace this call with joy, knowing it leads to true life in You.

Lord, give us the strength to deny ourselves, to take up our cross, and to follow You each day. Teach us to let go of our need for control, our fear of the unknown, and our attachment to the things of this world. May we find our life in You as we willingly die to ourselves.

We ask for Your Holy Spirit to guide us in this daily surrender. Help us to be aware of the moments when we need to die to our flesh and to choose life in the Spirit instead. Fill us with Your peace and joy as we walk in obedience to Your will.

Father, we pray for a heart of humility, that we would place Your desires above our own and seek Your glory in all we do. As we die daily, may we be renewed inwardly, growing in grace and becoming more like Jesus each day.

Thank You, Lord, for the promise of new life in You. We trust that as we surrender to Your will, You will lead us into the abundant life that You have prepared for us. In Jesus' name, Amen.

Day 26

Morning Devotion: Healing From The Inside Out

"He heals the brokenhearted and binds up their wounds." –Psalm 147:3 (NIV)

We often think of healing as something that happens on the outside—when a wound closes, a sickness is cured, or a pain subsides. But God's healing goes much deeper than the physical. He heals from the inside out, tending to the wounds of our hearts, minds, and spirits.

In Psalm 147:3, we are reminded that God heals the brokenhearted and binds up their wounds. This verse speaks to God's tender care for those who are hurting internally. Whether it's emotional pain from past hurts, the weight of grief, or the burden of anxiety, God is near to heal and restore.

For years, I walked around with a broken heart, bleeding on others, not understanding the magnitude of my sickness. All I knew was that I didn't feel good. Depression, oppression, and anxiety gripped my soul all while I was living everyday life. It wasn't until I found myself in the back of an ambulance being rushed to the hospital that I realized the seriousness of my inward sickness. I had to face the truth; I needed God to heal me from within.

The journey of healing from the inside out often begins with acknowledging our need for God's touch. It's easy to focus on the external symptoms of our pain, but true healing requires us to go deeper. We must bring our brokenness before God, trusting that He understands our pain and is able to heal us completely.

God's healing is not just about removing pain but about bringing wholeness. He wants to heal every part of us—our thoughts, emotions, and spirits—so that we can live in the fullness of life He has promised. This process might take time and may require us to confront difficult memories or feelings. But as we invite God into these places, we will experience His gentle, loving care.

Healing from the inside out also involves letting go of what holds us back—unforgiveness, bitterness, fear, or shame. These things can keep us from experiencing the full measure of God's healing. As we release them to God, He frees us from their hold and fills us with His peace and love.

As you begin this day, invite God to heal you from the inside out. Ask Him to touch the areas of your life that need His restoration. Trust in His promise to bind up your wounds and make you whole.

Let's Pray:

Heavenly Father, thank You for being the healer of our hearts, minds, and spirits. Today, we come before You with our brokenness, knowing that You are the only one who can bring true healing. We ask You to heal us from the inside out, touching the deepest parts of our being that are in need of Your restoration.

Lord, we surrender our pain, fears, and burdens to You. We ask for Your peace to fill our hearts, for Your love to cover our wounds, and for Your strength to sustain us as we walk this healing journey. Help us trust in Your timing and be patient as You work in us.

We also pray for the courage to let go of anything that hinders our healing—unforgiveness, bitterness, or fear. Teach us to release these things into Your hands, knowing that You are able to transform our pain into peace.

Thank You for Your faithfulness, Lord. We trust in Your promise to heal the brokenhearted and bind our wounds. May we walk in the fullness of the life You have for us, whole and restored by Your love. In Jesus' name, Amen.

Life Or Death Is In My Mouth

"Death and life are in the power of the tongue, and those who love it and indulge it will eat its fruit and bear the consequences of their words." —Proverbs 18:21 (AMP)

Words carry immense weight. The Bible reminds us that the tongue, though small, wields great power. It can speak life or death, build up or tear down, heal or wound. Every word we utter sets something in motion. This truth is echoed not only in Scripture but also in everyday experience—relationships, work-places, and communities are shaped by the words we choose.

In this passage, "death" and "life" represent the two extreme ends of the influence our words can have. Our words can create life, encouraging and nurturing others, breathing hope into a hopeless situation. Words can also destroy, diminish, and cause irreversible harm. A simple criticism can tear down a person's self-esteem, while a word of encouragement can spark confidence and belief. The choice lies in how we use this tool. Do we speak words that bring life, or do we, sometimes even unintentionally, speak words that cause damage? As followers of Christ, our calling is clear—to be a source of life through our words.

The verse reveals that we will bear the consequences of our words. When we consistently choose to speak life, we harvest good fruit. We build stronger relationships, foster unity, and experience the joy of seeing others uplifted. However, if we allow our tongues to be careless, critical, or cruel, we eventually eat the bitter fruit of division, broken trust, and regret.

This concept of "fruit" reminds us that every word spoken is a seed planted. Your words are seeds, and the atmosphere is soil. The harvest may not be immediate, but over time, what we sow with our words will grow and produce either life or destruction. Let's decide today to speak life!

Let's Pray:

Father, thank You for reminding us of the power of our words. Forgive us, Lord, for the times when we have spoken carelessly, allowing harmful words to escape our lips. Forgive us for the times we spoke out of frustration, anger, or insecurity, causing pain to those around us. We ask for Your mercy and grace to cover our shortcomings.

Lord, we recognize that every word we speak is like a seed planted, and we ask for Your wisdom to plant words of life, encouragement, and truth in every conversation we have. Fill our hearts with kindness so that our speech reflects Your love. Where there has been bitterness, resentment, negativity, or doubt within us, we ask You to uproot those things and replace them with a heart of faith that seeks to bless and edify others. Let our words be seasoned with grace to bring comfort, peace, and healing to those who hear them.

Teach us, Lord, to be slow to speak and quick to listen. Help us to pause in moments of conflict or stress so that we can respond with words guided by Your Spirit rather than by our emotions. Guard our tongues against speaking words in haste, anger, or fear. Let our speech be a reflection of faith, hope, and patience. In Jesus' name, Amen.

Day 28

Morning Devotion: Salty Enough

"You are the salt of the earth. But if the salt loses its saltiness, how can it be made salty again? It is no longer good for anything, except to be thrown out and trampled underfoot." – Matthew 5:13 (NIV)

My wife is one of the most amazing cooks that I know. When it comes to soul food, I would put her up against anybody. One thing I've noticed about her cooking (unless we're on a health kick) is that she adds salt to everything. In my opinion, there's something about salt that makes the food taste right. Most people would agree that when food has no salt, it tastes bland.

Well, this morning, I want you to see yourself as salt. Wherever you work, go to school, or live in your neighborhood, you are not there just to be there. God has placed you there to be the salt. Don't allow difficult situations to change who you are. If there is confusion, be the salt and let peace take control of the atmosphere. If someone is down, be the salt and give them a word of encouragement. If someone is lost in sin, be intentional about being the salt and show them the love of God. You are called to be the difference, even if that group, employer, company, or community doesn't know it yet. You don't have to make a big announcement—just be you. They will soon recognize that your presence brings something supernatural into the atmosphere. They may start saying things like, "You have such good energy," or "Things are better when you're around." But you'll know it's the salt—the God in you. You will know that it's His spirit living on the inside of you that brings flavor to whoever or whatever you connect with.

Let your day be filled with opportunities for God to pour you out like a salt shaker, and may you be salty enough!

Let's Pray:

Heavenly Father, thank You for calling us to be the salt of the earth. We are called to be a difference. Lord, just as salt enhances flavor, enable us to enhance the lives of those around us through acts of kindness. May our actions reflect Your love and grace, bringing comfort and hope to those who need it most. When we are tempted to conform to the world, remind us of our call to be different, to be 'salty.' Help us stand firm in who You've called us to be, regardless of the situations we face. No matter how difficult it is, help us not to relent. Help us to live in such a way that our life points others to You. Let Your peace flow through us when there is confusion. Let it bring a sense of calmness and tranquility. Give us the right words to say so that others may grow in confidence in who you are. Let your encouragement flow through us when others are down.

Help us to show Your love and grace to those who need it most. Help us to see others through Your eyes, recognizing the image of God in every person we encounter. Teach us to be patient, kind, and understanding, even when it's difficult. May our words and actions reflect the love of Christ, and may we always be quick to extend mercy and forgiveness.

Pour us out as vessels of Your supernatural presence. Let us be sensitive to the leading of the Holy Spirit, ready to speak a word of life, offer a helping hand, or be present for someone in need. May we be the difference in every room we enter, every situation we find ourselves in, and every life we touch. Let our lives be a testimony of Your goodness, drawing others closer to You. And Lord, when we falter or lose our way, when our 'saltiness' seems to fade, draw us back to You. Renew our spirit and rekindle our passion for Your ways.

As we go about our day, may we never forget that we are the salt of the earth, called to influence the world for Your glory.

In Jesus' name, Amen.

Day 29

Morning Devotion: The Ultimate Source Of Help

"I will lift up mine eyes unto the hills, from whence cometh my help. My help cometh from the Lord, which made heaven and earth."
−Psalm 121:1–2 (KJV)

God certainly gives us mentors, leaders, and coaches. A big shout-out to all who have been and are in my life. However, one day, I needed something, and I called a mentor, and I somewhat felt disregarded. I am so glad that happened at that moment. I realized I had an unfair and unrealistic expectation of them, their ability, and their time. Of course, I was not pastoring then and didn't understand this at first. However, I have learned that people often become disgruntled when they seek a connection with an individual that only God can give. Stop having unrealistic and unfair expectations of people.

Remember, in His presence is the fullness of everything you need. Get back to allowing Him to lead you, give you directions, and download strategies into your spirit. Following His plan works every time, and though we have one another, it is in Him that we live, move, and have our being. May you remember this as you go about your day—though people can assist us, real help comes from the Lord.

Let's Pray:

Father, we come today with humble hearts, asking for Your strength to lean into You more deeply. We thank You for the mentors, leaders, coaches, and friends You have placed in our lives to guide us, but we acknowledge that no one can ever replace You. You are our ultimate source of wisdom, strength, and help. Teach us to rely on You above all else. Help us to release any unrealistic expectations we've placed on others and redirect our hearts to trust fully in Your presence. May we never forget that You alone know our needs perfectly and provide for us in ways that no human ever could. Lead us, Lord, with Your divine guidance, and help us follow Your plan, for it is always perfect.

Father, fill us with Your peace when we feel disappointed or let down by others, reminding us that You never fail us. Give us clarity when we seek direction and strategies for every decision we face. Help us recognize that in You, we have everything we need—our fulfillment, purpose, and being come from You alone. We ask that You pour out Your wisdom on us, granting us discernment to know when to seek counsel from others and when to rest in Your presence.

Help us, Lord, to be patient when You ask us to wait, to trust in Your timing, and to understand that Your ways are higher than ours. Give us the courage to surrender control and the faith to walk in obedience even when the path seems unclear. Lord, help us see others through Your eyes, with grace and understanding, knowing they are also on their own journey with You.

Remove any bitterness or frustration from our hearts when we feel unmet in our expectations, and replace it with a deeper trust in Your sufficiency.

Today, we declare that we will lift our eyes to You, the maker of heaven and earth, for You are our helper and sustainer. May Your presence be our refuge and strength, and may Your love surround us, guiding our steps, healing our hearts, and equipping us to fulfill Your will in every area of our lives. Thank You, Lord, for being our source of everything. May we walk in the confidence that You are always with us, guiding, providing, and sustaining us in every season. We love and honor You. In the mighty name of Jesus, we pray, Amen.

Morning Devotion: Strength In All Circumstances

"I can do all things through Christ who strengthens me." –Philippians 4:13 (KJV)

Philippians 4:13 is a familiar verse and one of my favorites. Christians often quote it when facing big tasks, completing significant assignments, or accomplishing major goals. While this verse definitely applies to those situations, it's equally powerful in the context of life's storms—the battles that seem so hard, the rough or even hostile areas of our lives.

How about using this verse to support you in those challenging areas? I'm referring to the hostile environments in your home, at your job, or wherever your feet may tread. You can do all things through Christ. In other words, because of Christ, I will make it through this. I will not lose my character with my spouse, children, or boss. I will not fall to temptations because of the hostility around me. I will not be oppressed by hostile circumstances. Why? Because Christ strengthens me and gives me the power to overcome.

Hostility is defined as unfriendliness or opposition, and we will encounter these things in life. I recall a season when it seemed like I faced hostility in every area of my life, especially my work environment. And yes, I went to God about it so many times. I would often share with my husband, and we united in prayer for God to move on my behalf. However, I soon learned that no matter how inconvenient it seemed, most times, hostility could not be avoided. I also had to learn that no matter how unfair and unjust the treatment was, I was responsible for denying my flesh, opinions, and feelings. I was responsible for giving it to God so that he could handle it the right way. Ultimately, I had a responsibility to be spiritually mature.

My question to you is, "How will you respond?" Ultimately, your response is your responsibility. Will you depend on Christ and allow His strength to be perfect in your weakness, or will you succumb to the hostilities in life?

I encourage you to lean into the strength of God.

Let's Pray:

Lord, we thank You for a heart of love and not hate. We come against feelings of bitterness and strife. We pull and cast down enviousness and the spirit of retaliation. Remove every need to justify and validate ourselves because You are our advocate and redeemer. You are our shield; You protect us.

Lord, even though You said in Your Word that vengeance is Yours, and You will repay, remove the need in us to see others dealt with for coming against us. Because while You were on the cross, in the middle of Your crucifixion, at the most painful time of suffering, Jesus, You said, "Forgive them, for they know not what they do." So, even during the time of personal crucifixion, help us to forgive and examine ourselves so that only Your love will manifest in us so that we can count ourselves blameless, not in false humility, but in total surrender to You.

Help us to wait on You because faith worketh patience, and faith only works through Your love. So, Lord, thank You for allowing everything we go through to make us more like You. We receive Your strength today. In Jesus' name, Amen.

Day 31

Morning Devotion: First Things First

"But seek first the kingdom of God and His righteousness, and all these things shall be added to you." –Matthew 6:33 (NKJV)

In a world filled with distractions and demands, it's easy to let our priorities become misaligned. We often find ourselves chasing after things that seem urgent but may not be truly important at the end of the day. However, Jesus gives us a clear directive in Matthew 6:33: *"But seek first the kingdom of God and His righteousness, and all these things shall be added to you."*

This verse calls us to focus our hearts and minds on what truly matters—God's kingdom and His righteousness. When we put God first, everything else falls into its proper place. Jesus assures us that when we prioritize God, He will provide for our needs.

What does it mean to "seek first" the Kingdom of God? It means prioritizing our relationship with Him above all else. It means aligning our lives with His will and trusting Him to take care of the details. Instead of worrying about the future or striving for material things, we must focus on our spiritual growth and obedience to God's Word.

Seeking God first also involves dedicating time each day to

prayer, reading the Bible, and reflecting on His promises. It's about making God the center of our lives, not just someone we turn to in times of trouble. When we seek Him first, we are reminded of His love, power, and faithfulness.

As we put God first, we experience a sense of peace that transcends our circumstances. Our faith is strengthened, and our trust in God's provision grows. The things that once caused us anxiety or stress become less significant because we know that God is in control.

As you go through your day, ask yourself: *Am I seeking God first in my decisions, actions, and thoughts?* Take time to realign your priorities and ensure that God is at the center of everything you do. Remember, when you seek Him first, He promises to take care of all your needs.

Let's Pray:

Heavenly Father, we come before You with grateful hearts, acknowledging Your greatness and our need for Your guidance in our lives. Thank You for the gift of a new day and the opportunity to seek You first.

Lord, we ask for Your help in prioritizing You above all else. In the midst of our busy lives and the constant flow of distractions, help us to keep our focus on You. Teach us to seek Your kingdom and righteousness in every aspect of our day, and remind us of the promise that when we do, You will take care of everything else.

Grant us the strength to resist the lure of distractions that pull us away from our time with You. Whether it's the demands of work, the pressures of daily responsibilities, or the noise of the world, help us set aside time each day to be with You, pray, and meditate on Your Word.

We ask for Your wisdom to recognize and avoid the things that lead us away from Your presence. Help us make intentional choices that reflect our commitment to putting You first. When we feel overwhelmed or tempted to skip our time with You, remind us of the peace and clarity that come from seeking You.

Father, fill our hearts with a deep desire for Your presence. Let our mornings begin with Your guidance, and our days be carried out in Your strength. As we start each day, may we do so with a heart eager to seek You, knowing You are faithful to guide us and provide for all our needs.

We thank You for Your unwavering love and faithfulness. May our lives reflect our commitment to You and Your kingdom. Help us live each day with purpose, focused on honoring You in all we do. In Jesus' name, Amen.